People

Growing up

Elizabeth Paren and
Gill Stacey

Oxford University Press

Do you remember when you were a baby?

You have grown up a lot since then.

This book tells you about growing up.

Contents

A new baby

This family is getting ready for
a new baby.
The baby is growing inside the
mother's womb.

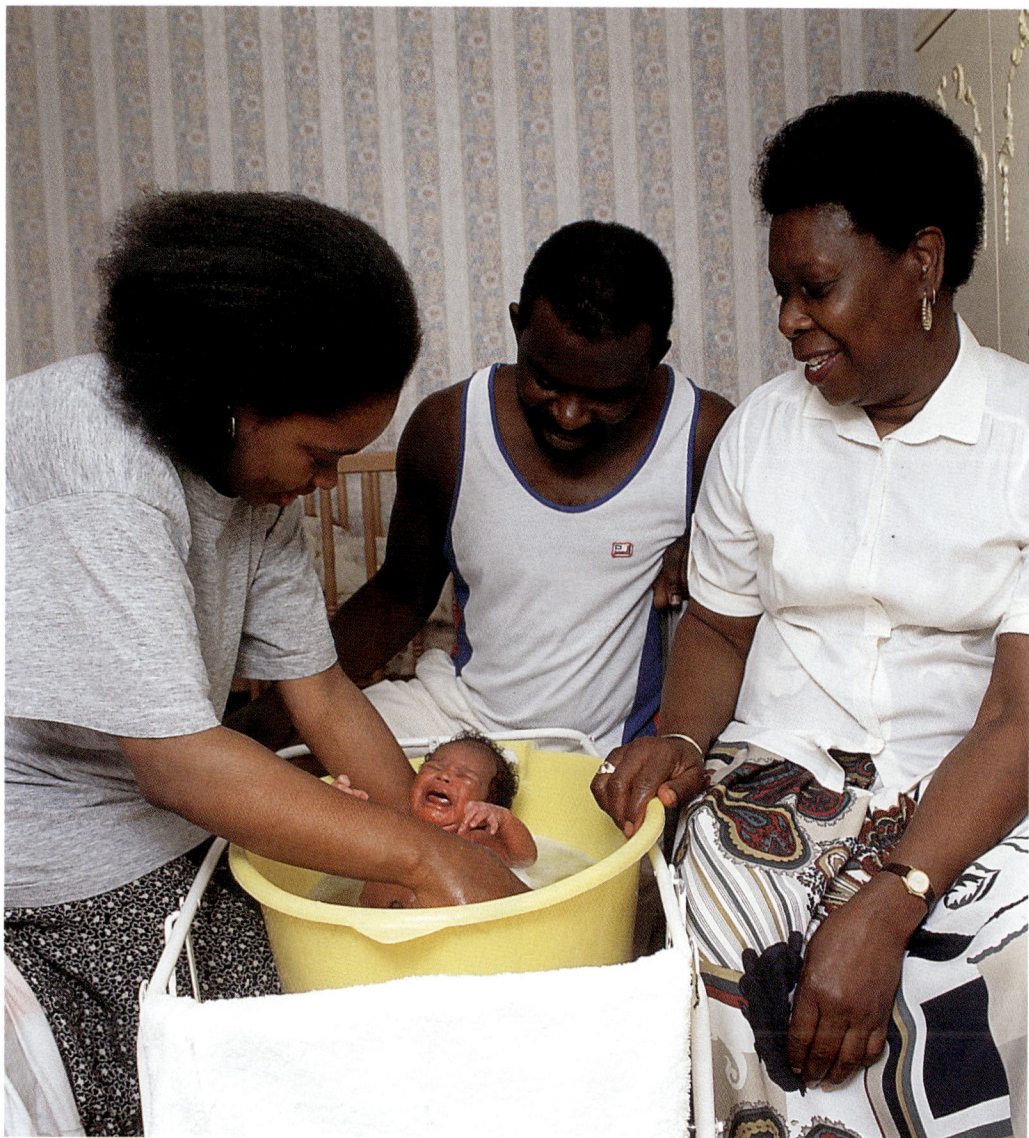

A tiny baby can kick.

He can hold on to things.

But he cannot hold his head up.

A baby grows

first teeth

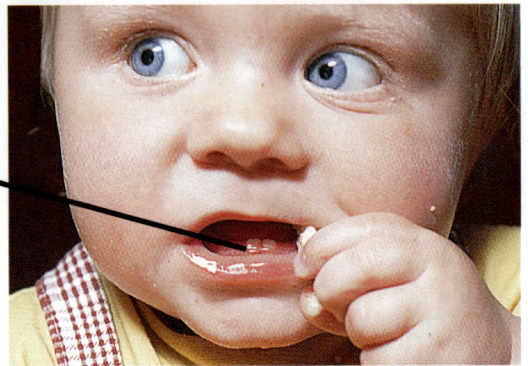

A baby grows quickly.

At first, she only drinks milk.

As she grows, she needs different foods.

Her first teeth help her to chew.

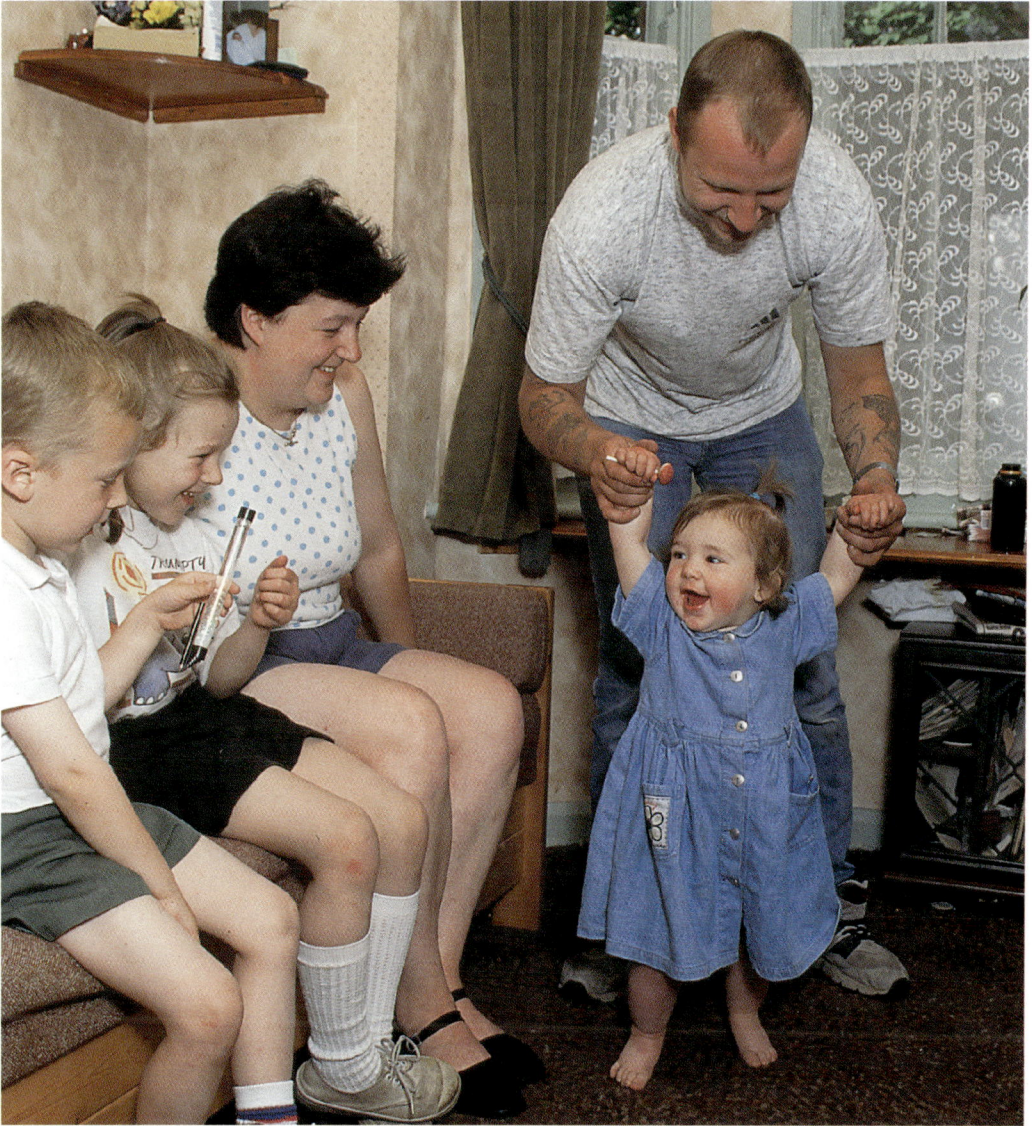

This baby is growing bigger and stronger.

She is walking for the first time.

Playing and learning

This boy is learning to talk.

Young children learn all the time.

This girl is learning about shapes.

This girl is writing about when
she was a baby.
She has changed and grown a
lot since then.

Growing and changing

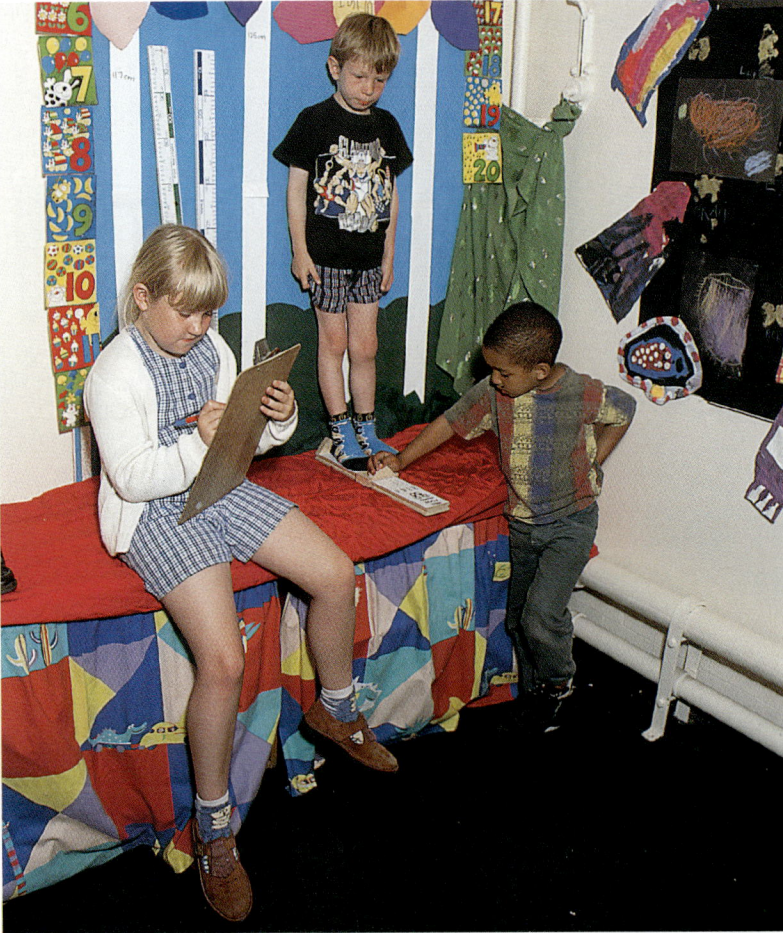

These children are finding out
how people grow.
They are all the same age.
But they are not all the same size.

Exercise helps children to
grow up strong and healthy.

Growing up

These girls are buying their own clothes.
They are teenagers.
They are almost grown-up.

These students are sixteen.

They are working very hard.

At weekends, they like to go out with their friends.

Grown-up

This young man is grown-up now.
He is old enough to leave home.

People stop growing taller.

But they do not stop changing.

They can go on learning all their lives.

Index

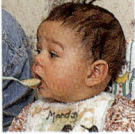 

Oxford University Press, Great Clarendon Street,
Oxford OX2 6DP
© Oxford University Press
All rights reserved

First published by Oxford University Press 1997

ISBN 0 19 916938 1

Available in packs
People Pack (one of each title)
ISBN 0 19 916942 X
People Class Pack (six of each title)
ISBN 0 19 916943 8

Acknowledgements

Illustrated by: Alex Brychta (p2).

All photographs are by kind permission of John Birdsall.

Cover photograph: Martin Sookias.

Printed and bound in Hong Kong